Slow Cooker Recipe Book UK

Quick, Healthy and Amazing Dishes for
Every Day incl. Sides, Desserts & More

Sara Garfield

ISBN - 9798354357819

Table of Contens

EXCLUSIVE BONUS

40 Weight Loss Recipes

&

14 Days Meal Plan

Scan the QR-Code and receive
the FREE download:

Introduction

What Is a Slow Cooker?

A slow cooker is a countertop appliance used to simmer food at low cooking temperatures over long periods of time. You should not be surprised to see a slow cooker recipe with cooking times of several hours. One of the main benefits of slow cookers is the long cooking times as it allows for hands-free cooking. You can prepare and put your ingredients in the pot, leave home and come back to a delicious, freshly prepared meal.

The average slow cooker also uses less power than an oven, using just enough electrical energy to maintain the heat or set temperature. Slow cookers operate using a low 120W, just slightly more energy than a 100W light bulb. Whereas, ovens use about 220W of electricity, small hobs use about 300W, and large hobs require about 1,500W. Slow cookers can not only save you time spent in the kitchen but only reduce your bills. Slow cookers are an economical cooking option for many families.

Typically, slow cookers consist of a ceramic or porcelain pot completely surrounded by an electrical unit with a heating element. A lid, typically of glass, is placed on top of the pot to create a seal which traps the moisture generated from the food as it is heated. Slow cookers gently cook food slowly by maximizing the high heat capacity of the moisture trapped in the pot.

Despite long cooking times, slow cookers will not dry out your food and will instead retain more of its juices. This makes slow cookers great for stews, soups, and sauces. They are especially suited for cheaper cuts of meat which become perfectly tender and delicious when cooked in a slow cooker. There are also many other recipes, including

drinks and desserts, that you can use a slow cooker for. As a bonus, we have also included a 30-day slow cooker meal plan with shopping lists to make life even easier. Slow cookers are very versatile appliances, the recipes in this book will make sure you get the most out of yours.

Benefits of Using Slow Cookers

- ✍ Hands-free cooking
- ✍ Safe to leave on all day
- ✍ Saves cooking time and energy
- ✍ Portable
- ✍ Easy to set up and use
- ✍ Easy to clean and less used pots and pans
- ✍ Used for many meal types
- ✍ The low setting keeps food warm ahead of meal time

What's the Best Slow Cooker to Buy?

As the number of households using slow cookers has risen, so has the number of different types of slow cookers for you to choose from. You can find slow cookers from all the popular household kitchen appliance brands, varying in price. Round slow cookers tend to be cheaper and take up less countertop space. Oval slow cookers tend to be larger, allowing enough space for bulky food, such as a whole chicken or pork chops. All slow cookers work in similar ways but differ in features and quality.

You may find a programmable timer to be handy and give you some reassurance if you are away from home. Although, digital slow cookers are more expensive than basic models which are operated manually and with few settings. Most slow cookers have at least two heat settings, low or high. Both can be used for cooking and the low setting can also be used to keep food warm before serving. Some slow cookers have an auto

setting which starts the cooker on high for several hours and then switches to low until the setting is changed. An indicator light is also an important feature to prevent you from wasting time and food if there is an unexpected power outage.

When looking for a slow cooker for your kitchen, you must first decide on the size or capacity that will suit your needs. The size of the slow cooker does not equate to the amount of food it can cook. Around two-thirds of the stated volume can be used for cooking as you cannot fill the cooking pot to the top.

The most popular size slow cooker is 3-4.5 litre, suited for a couple or small family. Larger families will need a 5-6.5 litre slow cooker. Large slow cookers have enough capacity for bulk cooking, as you can freeze extra food or leftovers to serve again. A 1.5-3 litre slow cooker is also handy if you host many gatherings or parties as it is perfect for serving sides, snacks, dips, etc.

Slow Cooker Size Guide

Size	Capacity
1.5-3 litre	1-2 people
3-5 litre	3-4 people
5-6.5 litre	5+ people

How Do You Use a Slow Cooker?

Using a slow cooker couldn't be easier. Once you have prepared your ingredients, you add them into the cooking pot sitting in the slow cooker, add the lid, set the heat setting, and let the slow cooker do the rest. Generally, it does not matter what order the ingredients go. Further details for slow-cooking specific foods are found below. Assume a 3-5 litre slow cooker is used unless a specific size is stated in the recipe.

It is really important to never fill a slow cooker to the top. Leave at least 5 cm of space between the top of the cooking pot for simmering. Avoid removing the lid to check on the food. A glass lid allows you to look through if you need reassurance. Every time you lift the lid, heat is lost, therefore increasing the cooking time. It is not necessary to stir the food unless the recipe specifies.

If cooking cakes or breads, do not lift the lid during the first 1 ½ to 2 hours of cooking time. It is not recommended to cook frozen foods.

For food safety, defrost meat and vegetables completely before adding to the slow cookers.

The best results are achieved by cooking recipes with the low setting. The extra cooking time is more than worth it to get melt-in-your-mouth meals. If you are pressed for time or if a recipe calls for it, then use the higher heat setting.

If you are looking to swap out a conventional oven for a slow cooker in a given recipe then you will need to adjust the cooking times and amount of liquid used. Slow cookers will need less liquid as very little of the moisture escapes the pot. A recipe which calls for 6-8 hours of cooking time on the low setting will typically take 2-4 hours on the high setting. Cooking in the oven for 15-30 minutes will take 4-6 hours on low, or 1-2 hours on high, using a slow cooker.

Proper care and cleaning of your slow cooker will help you get the very best results for every meal you make. As all the ingredients are typically cooked in one pot, slow cookers save you time and effort washing several different pots and pans. Before starting to clean your slow cooker, be sure it is off, unplugged, and has been left to cool. Lids and removable cooking pots can be cleaned with hot, soapy water or in a dishwasher. Avoid using scouring pads or abrasive cleaners as they can scratch and damage the pot. Instead, use sponges or cloths. To remove grease and stubborn stains, soak in vinegar and rinse in water. Never immerse the heating element in water. Slow cooker liners can also be used to easily clean up spills as they are thrown away after use.

Tips For Slow-Cooking Specific Foods

Meats - Tougher, larger cuts of meat, such as beef rump or pork shoulder, are perfect for long, slow cooking. Minced meats need to be browned and crumbled with a fork before added to the slow cooker to prevent from clumping. Other cuts of meat do not need browning, saving you time and leaving less pots and pans to wash up.

Vegetables - Vegetables with higher water content, such as squash or zucchini, cook more quickly than root vegetables, such as carrots, so cut them into large pieces and add them to the slow cooker during the last 30 minutes of cooking time.

Frozen vegetables - Thaw before adding to the slow cooker during the last 15 to 20 minutes of cooking time to prevent them from overcooking.

Seafood - Add pieces of fish (cod, salmon, haddock, etc.) and shellfish (clams, shrimp, scallops, etc.) during the last 10 to 15 minutes of cooking time.

Liquids (stock, water, wine) - Liquids help with heat transfer to ensure your food is evenly cooked. When doubling recipes for stews multiply the volume of liquid by 1.5.

Pasta - Dried pasta should be cooked al dente and added to the slow cooker during the last 15 to 20 minutes of cooking time. Small soup pasta, such as stelline or orzo can be added, uncooked, during the last 20 to 30 minutes of cooking time. Fresh pasta can be added, uncooked, during the last 15 to 20 minutes of cooking time.

Rice - Only long-grain rice cooks well in a slow cooker. Be sure there is plenty of liquid in the pot and add the uncooked rice during the last 1 ½ to 2 hours of cooking time. Other types of rice, such as brown or basmati, should be cooked and added near the end of cooking time.

Dried beans and lentils - Dried beans do not need to be presoaked and will cook in stews and soups with plenty of liquid in 7 to 8 hours on the high setting. Acid ingredients, such as tomatoes and vinegar, prevent beans from becoming tender. Add them near the

end of cooking time once the beans are tender. Dried lentils do not require presoaking and can be added at the beginning of cooking time.

Dairy - Full-fat dairy products don't curdle as easily as lower fat milk products. The following recipes call for any semi-skimmed milk to be added towards the end of the cooking time with cornstarch to prevent curdling.

Herbs - Add ground and dried herbs at the beginning of the cooking time, adding more to taste at the end, if needed. Add fresh herbs at the end for optimal colour and flavour.

Thickeners - Cornstarch and flour can be added to thicken stews and soups. The following recipes use cornstarch as it thickens more quickly and doesn't affect the taste of the food.

Slow Cooker Do's & Don'ts

Do's

- ❧ Brown large cuts of meat before adding to your slow cooker.
- ❧ Thaw frozen ingredients overnight in the refrigerator before adding to your slow cooker.
- ❧ Add foods that take longer to cook to the bottom of the cooking pot. Pour liquids last.
- ❧ Follow recipes carefully.
- ❧ Use oven mitts to remove the cooking pot at the end of the cooking time.

Don'ts

- ❧ Overfill your slow cooker.
- ❧ Remove the lid or stir during cooking unless stated in the recipe.
- ❧ Reheat or store leftovers in a slow cooker.
- ❧ Use abrasive sponges or cleaners to clean the cooking pot.

Recipes

BEEF

FAMILY BEEF STEW

TIME: 6-8 HOURS | SERVES 4
NET CARBS: 29.7G | FAT: 6.6G
PROTEIN: 26G | KCAL: 292

INGREDIENTS

- 500g beef round steak, cut into strips
- 250ml reduced-sodium fat-free beef broth
- 125ml dry red wine or beef broth
- 320g cut green beans
- 2 each: cubed medium potatoes, small onions cut into wedges
- 3 carrots, thickly sliced
- 3/4 teaspoon dried thyme leaves
- Salt and pepper, to taste

INSTRUCTIONS

1. Combine all ingredients, except salt and pepper, in a slow cooker.
2. Cover and cook on low for 6 to 8 hours.
3. Season to taste with salt and pepper.

GREEK BEEF AND LENTIL STEW

TIME: 6-8 HOURS | SERVES 6
NET CARBS: 46.7G | FAT: 3.4G
PROTEIN: 25.5G | KCAL: 302

INGREDIENTS

- 500g cubed boneless beef
- 750ml reduced-sodium fat-free beef broth
- 5 cans (400g each) diced tomatoes, undrained
- 280g cubed potatoes
- 300g cut green beans
- 190g dried lentils
- 50g chopped onion
- 150g green bell pepper
- 2 teaspoons minced garlic
- 1 teaspoon each: dried oregano and mint leaves
- 1/2 teaspoon each: ground turmeric, coriander
- 125g cubed zucchini
- Salt and pepper, to taste

INSTRUCTIONS

1. Combine all ingredients, except zucchini, salt, and pepper, in a 5 - 6.5 L slow cooker.
2. Cover and cook on low for 6 to 8 hours.
3. Add zucchini during the last 30 minutes.
4. Season to taste with salt and pepper.

CHILI CON CARNE

TIME: 6-8 HOURS | SERVES 8
NET CARBS: 28.7G | FAT: 4.6G
PROTEIN: 21.9G | KCAL: 220

INGREDIENTS

- 450g lean minced beef
- 50g chopped onions
- 150g green bell pepper
- 2 cloves garlic, minced
- 1–2 tablespoons chili powder
- 2 teaspoons each: ground cumin, dried oregano leaves
- 2 cans (400g each) diced tomatoes, undrained
- 1 can (400g) red kidney beans, rinsed, drained
- 1 can (170g) tomato paste
- 170ml beer or water
- 1 tablespoon each: packed light brown sugar, unsweetened cocoa
- Salt and pepper, to taste
- 60g shredded reduced-fat Cheddar cheese
- 25g sliced green onions
- 120g reduced-fat sour cream

INSTRUCTIONS

1. Cook minced beef in a lightly greased large skillet over medium heat until meat is browned for about 10 minutes, crumbling with a fork.
2. Combine beef and remaining ingredients, except salt, pepper, cheese, green onions, and sour cream, in a slow cooker.
3. Cover and cook on low for 6 to 8 hours.
4. Season to taste with salt and pepper.
5. Sprinkle each bowl of chili with cheese, green onions, and sour cream.

TACO CHILI

TIME: 6-8 HOURS | SERVES 8
NET CARBS: 31.3G | FAT: 5.6G
PROTEIN: 17G | KCAL: 301

INGREDIENTS

- 250–500g lean minced beef
- 1 can (400g) kidney beans, rinsed, drained
- 2 cans (400g each) diced tomatoes, undrained
- 165g sweetcorn, drained
- 1 large onion, chopped
- 2 ribs celery, chopped
- 1 pack taco seasoning mix
- 1 pack ranch seasoning mix
- Garnishes: sour cream, shredded Cheddar cheese, taco chips

INSTRUCTIONS

1. Cook minced beef in a lightly greased large skillet until browned, for about 10 minutes, crumbling with a fork.
2. Combine beef and remaining ingredients, except garnishes, in a slow cooker.
3. Cover and cook on low for 6 to 8 hours.
4. Serve with garnishes.

BEEF AND VEGETABLE STEW

TIME: 6-8 HOURS | SERVES 6
NET CARBS: 35.9G | FAT: 5.5G
PROTEIN: 24.5G | KCAL: 289

INGREDIENTS

- 3kg lean beef round steak, cubed
- 250ml reduced-sodium fat-free beef broth
- 125ml red wine or beef broth
- 6 medium carrots, quartered
- 4 each: quartered small potatoes, onions
- 2 small zucchini, sliced
- 100g small mushrooms
- 1 clove garlic, minced
- 1 teaspoon Worcestershire sauce
- 2 bay leaves
- 1 tablespoon cornstarch
- 50ml cold water
- Salt and pepper, to taste

INSTRUCTIONS

1. Combine all ingredients, except cornstarch, water, salt, and pepper, in a 5 - 6.5 L slow cooker.
2. Cover and cook on low for 6 to 8 hours.
3. Turn heat to high and cook for 10 minutes.
4. Stir in combined cornstarch and water, stirring for 2 to 3 minutes.
5. Discard bay leaves.
6. Season to taste with salt and pepper.

BEEF STROGANOFF

TIME: 6-8 HOURS | SERVES 6
NET CARBS: 45.1G | FAT: 12.2G
PROTEIN: 39G | KCAL: 423

INGREDIENTS

- 500g lean beef eye of round or sirloin steak, cut into strips
- 250ml reduced-sodium fat-free beef broth
- 300g sliced mushrooms
- 30g sliced onion
- 2 cloves garlic, minced
- 1 teaspoon Dijon mustard
- 1/2 teaspoon dried thyme leaves
- 125ml reduced-fat sour cream
- 1 tablespoon cornstarch
- Salt and pepper, to taste
- 225g cooked noodles, warm

INSTRUCTIONS

1. Combine all ingredients, except sour cream, cornstarch, salt, pepper, and noodles, in a slow cooker.
2. Cover and cook on low for 6 to 8 hours.
3. Stir in combined sour cream and cornstarch, stirring for 2 to 3 minutes.
4. Season to taste with salt and pepper.
5. Serve over noodles.

HEARTY MEATBALL & VEGGIE STEW

TIME: 6-8 HOURS | SERVES 6
NET CARBS: 65.3G | FAT: 21.8G
PROTEIN: 35.8G | KCAL: 554

INGREDIENTS

- Hearty Meatballs (recipe follows)
- 250ml reduced-sodium fat-free beef broth
- 2 cans (400g each) diced tomatoes, undrained
- 3 carrots, thickly sliced
- 1 teaspoon dried basil leaves
- 2 small zucchini, sliced
- 115g frozen peas, thawed
- 2 tablespoons cornstarch
- 50ml cold water
- Salt and pepper, to taste
- 350g noodles, cooked, warm

INSTRUCTIONS

1. Combine all ingredients, except zucchini, peas, cornstarch, water, salt, pepper, and noodles, in a slow cooker, making sure meatballs are submerged.
2. Cover and cook on low for 6 to 8 hours, adding zucchini and peas during the last 20 minutes.
3. Turn heat to high and cook for 10 minutes.
4. Stir in combined cornstarch and water, stirring for 2 to 3 minutes.
5. Season to taste with salt and pepper.
6. Serve over noodles.

HEARTY MEATBALLS

MAKES 18

INGREDIENTS

- 3kg lean minced beef
- 50g finely chopped onion
- 1 egg
- 60g unseasoned dry bread crumbs
- 2 cloves garlic, minced
- 1–2 teaspoons beef-flavor bouillon crystals
- 1/2 teaspoon salt
- 1/4 teaspoon pepper

INSTRUCTIONS

1. Mix all ingredients in a bowl.
2. Shape mixture into 18 meatballs.

PHILLY CHEESE STEAK SANDWICHES

TIME: 6-8 HOURS | SERVES 6-8
NET CARBS: 43.6G | FAT: 8.3G
PROTEIN: 2.3G | KCAL: 568

INGREDIENTS

- 500g boneless round steak, thinly sliced
- 115g thinly sliced onion
- 115g green bell pepper,
- 150ml reduced-sodium beef broth
- 1 teaspoon minced garlic
- 1 tablespoon Worcestershire sauce
- Salt and pepper, to taste
- 6–8 hard or hoagie rolls
- 225g shredded reduced-fat mozzarella cheese

INSTRUCTIONS

1. Combine all ingredients, except salt, pepper, rolls, and cheese, in a slow cooker.
2. Cover and cook on low for 6 to 8 hours.
3. Season to taste with salt and pepper.
4. Top rolls with meat and vegetable mixture.
5. Sprinkle with cheese.
6. If desired, broil 15 cm from a heat source until the cheese is melted for 3 to 4 minutes.

ITALIAN BEEF SANDWICHES

TIME: 10-12 HOURS | SERVES 12
NET CARBS: 30.7G | FAT: 5.1G
PROTEIN: 23.6G | KCAL: 266

INGREDIENTS

- 1 boneless beef rump roast (about 1.4kg)
- 750ml beef broth
- 1 pack Italian salad dressing mix
- 1 bay leaf
- 1 teaspoon pepper
- 12 buns or Italian rolls

INSTRUCTIONS

1. Combine all ingredients, except buns, in a slow cooker.
2. Cover and cook on low for 10 to 12 hours.
3. Remove meat and shred.
4. Return to the slow cooker.
5. Serve meat and juices in buns.

SLOPPY JOES

TIME: 2-3 HOURS | SERVES 6-8
NET CARBS: 35.8G | FAT: 9.9G
PROTEIN: 19.1G | KCAL: 278

INGREDIENTS

- 500g minced beef
- 50g chopped onion
- 150g chopped green or red bell pepper
- 2 teaspoons minced garlic
- 235g ketchup
- 125ml cup water
- 50g packed light brown sugar
- 2 tablespoons prepared mustard
- 2 teaspoons each: celery seeds, chili powder
- Salt and pepper, to taste
- 6–8 whole-wheat hamburger buns, toasted
- 8 sweet or dill pickles

INSTRUCTIONS

1. Cook minced beef in a lightly greased skillet until browned, crumbling with a fork.
2. Combine minced beef and remaining ingredients, except salt, pepper, buns, and pickles, in a slow cooker.
3. Cover and cook on high for 2 to 3 hours.
4. Season to taste with salt and pepper.
5. Serve in buns with pickles.

CHICKEN

EASY CHICKEN STEW

TIME: 5-6 HOURS | SERVES 4
NET CARBS: 27G | FAT: 8.8G
PROTEIN: 34G | KCAL: 293

INGREDIENTS

- 3 cans (290g each) reduced-sodium 98% fat-free condensed cream of chicken soup
- 625ml semi-skimmed milk
- 250ml water
- 500g boneless, skinless chicken breasts, cubed
- 50g sliced onion
- 1 package (250g) frozen mixed vegetables, thawed
- 2 tablespoons cornstarch
- 50ml cold water
- Salt and pepper, to taste

INSTRUCTIONS

1. Combine soup, milk, and water in a slow cooker.
2. Stir in the chicken and onions.
3. Cover and cook on low for 5 to 6 hours, adding mixed vegetables during the last 20 minutes.
4. Turn heat to high and cook for 10 minutes.
5. Stir in combined cornstarch and water, stirring for 2 to 3 minutes.
6. Season to taste with salt and pepper.

HONEY-MUSTARD CHICKEN STEW

TIME: 4-5 HOURS | SERVES 4
NET CARBS: 28.6G | FAT: 4G
PROTEIN: 30.3G | KCAL: 276

INGREDIENTS

- 450g boneless, skinless chicken breast, cubed
- 750ml reduced-sodium fat-free chicken broth
- 130g small cauliflower florets
- 50g chopped onion
- 150g sliced carrots

- 2 tablespoons honey
- 1 tablespoon Dijon mustard
- 1–2 teaspoons curry powder
- 1–2 tablespoons cornstarch
- 2–4 tablespoons cold water
- Salt and pepper, to taste
- 600g cooked white rice, warm

INSTRUCTIONS

1. Combine all ingredients, except cornstarch, water, salt, pepper, and rice, in a slow cooker.
2. Cover and cook on high for 4 to 5 hours. Stir in combined cornstarch and water, stirring for 2 to 3 minutes.
3. Season to taste with salt and pepper.
4. Serve over rice.

CHICKEN AND MUSHROOM STEW

TIME: 4-6 HOURS | SERVES 4
NET CARBS: 41.4G | FAT: 2.6G
PROTEIN: 29.5G | KCAL: 338

INGREDIENTS

- 500g boneless, skinless chicken breast, cubed
- 250ml reduced-sodium fat-free chicken broth
- 1 can (170g) tomato paste
- 1 tablespoon Worcestershire sauce
- 75g mushrooms, thickly sliced
- 1 large onion, chopped
- 2 each: minced cloves garlic, coarsely shredded large carrots
- 1 bay leaf
- 1 teaspoon dried Italian seasoning
- 1/4 teaspoon dry mustard
- 1–2 tablespoons cornstarch
- 2–4 tablespoons cold water
- Salt and pepper, to taste
- 225g spaghetti, cooked, warm

INSTRUCTIONS

1. Combine all ingredients, except cornstarch, water, salt, pepper, and spaghetti, in a slow cooker.
2. Cover and cook on high for 4 to 6 hours.
3. Stir in combined cornstarch and water, stirring for 2 to 3 minutes.
4. Discard the bay leaf.
5. Season to taste with salt and pepper.
6. Serve over spaghetti.

CHICKEN AND MASHED POTATO STEW

TIME: 6-8 HOURS | SERVES 4
NET CARBS: 35.1G | FAT: 12.8G
PROTEIN: 29.9G | KCAL: 378

INGREDIENTS

- 500g boneless, skinless chicken breast, cubed
- 250ml reduced-sodium fat-free chicken broth
- 35g chopped onion
- 35g carrots
- 35g celery, sliced
- 35g mushrooms
- 1/2 teaspoon each: dried rosemary and thyme leaves
- 110g frozen peas, thawed
- 1–2 tablespoons cornstarch
- 3–4 tablespoons cold water
- Salt and pepper, to taste
- 3 cups Mashed Potatoes (recipe follows)
- 1 egg yolk
- 50g shredded reduced-fat Cheddar cheese
- 1–2 tablespoons margarine or butter, melted

INSTRUCTIONS

1. Combine chicken, broth, onion, carrots, celery, mushrooms, and herbs in a slow cooker.
2. Cover and cook on low for 6 to 8 hours.
3. Add peas, turn heat to high, and cook for 10 minutes.
4. Stir in combined cornstarch and water, stirring for 2 to 3 minutes.
5. Season to taste with salt and pepper.
6. While stew is cooking, make Mashed Potatoes, mixing in egg yolk and cheese.
7. Spoon potato mixture into 4 mounds on a greased cookie sheet and refrigerate, covered, for about 30 minutes, until chilled.
8. Drizzle potatoes with margarine.
9. Bake at 220 degrees until browned, for about 15 minutes.
10. Top bowls of stew with potatoes.

MASHED POTATOES

3 SERVINGS

INGREDIENTS

- 500g potatoes, peeled, cooked, warm
- 75ml semi-skimmed milk
- 80g sour cream
- 2 tablespoons margarine or butter
- Salt and pepper, to taste

INSTRUCTIONS

1. Mash potatoes or beat until smooth, adding milk, sour cream, and margarine.
2. Season to taste with salt and pepper.

TOMATO-CHICKEN STEW

TIME: 6-8 HOURS | SERVES 6
NET CARBS: 18.1G | FAT: 6.5G
PROTEIN: 32G | KCAL: 253

INGREDIENTS

- 3kg boneless, skinless chicken breast, cubed
- 1 can (400g) diced tomatoes, undrained
- 1 can (400g) cannellini beans, rinsed, drained
- 250ml reduced-sodium fat-free chicken broth
- 125ml cup dry white wine or chicken broth
- 60g tomato paste
- 200g sliced mushrooms
- 50g sliced onion
- 2 cloves garlic, minced
- 2 teaspoons lemon juice
- 1 bay leaf
- 1/2 teaspoon dried oregano leaves
- 1/4 teaspoon dried thyme leaves
- Salt and pepper, to taste

INSTRUCTIONS

1. Combine all ingredients, except salt and pepper, in a slow cooker.
2. Cover and cook on low for 6 to 8 hours.
3. Discard bay leaf.
4. Season to taste with salt and pepper.

LEMON CHICKEN STEW

TIME: 4-5 HOURS | SERVES 6
NET CARBS: 38.2G | FAT: 7.3G
PROTEIN: 26.2G | KCAL: 310

INGREDIENTS

- 500g boneless, skinless chicken breast, cubed
- 2 cans (400g each) diced tomatoes, undrained
- 1 jalapeño chili, minced
- 2 cloves garlic, minced
- 1 teaspoon instant chicken bouillon crystals
- 2 teaspoons dried basil leaves
- 200g broccoli florets
- 50–75ml lemon juice
- Salt and pepper, to taste
- 300g angel hair pasta, cooked, warm
- Shredded Parmesan cheese, as garnish

INSTRUCTIONS

1. Combine all ingredients, except broccoli, lemon juice, salt, pepper, pasta, and cheese, in a slow cooker.
2. Cover and cook on high for 4 to 5 hours, adding broccoli during the last 20 minutes.
3. Season to taste with lemon juice, salt, and pepper.
4. Serve over pasta.
5. Sprinkle with Parmesan cheese.

CLASSIC CHICKEN NOODLE SOUP

TIME: 4-6 HOURS | SERVES 4
NET CARBS: 44.3G | FAT: 5.8G
PROTEIN: 22.8G | KCAL: 307

INGREDIENTS

- 4 cans (400g each) reduced-sodium fat-free chicken broth
- 100g boneless, skinless chicken breast, cubed
- 100g skinless chicken thighs, cubed
- 130g sliced celery
- 50g carrots
- 50g chopped onion
- 1 teaspoon dried marjoram leaves
- 1 bay leaf
- 75g cooked wide noodles
- Salt and pepper, to taste

INSTRUCTIONS

1. Combine all ingredients, except noodles, salt, and pepper, in a slow cooker.
2. Cover and cook on high for 4 to 6 hours, adding noodles during the last 20 minutes.
3. Discard the bay leaf.
4. Season to taste with salt and pepper.

INDIAN CURRY CHICKEN AND VEGETABLE STEW

TIME: 6-8 HOURS | SERVES 6
NET CARBS: 76.7G | FAT: 9.6G
PROTEIN: 38.7G | KCAL: 509

INGREDIENTS

- 500g chicken breasts, halved
- 175ml reduced-sodium vegetable broth
- 175ml reduced-fat or regular coconut milk
- 1 can (400g) crushed tomatoes
- 60g tomato paste
- 200g mushrooms, coarsely chopped
- 140g cubed potato
- 115g sliced carrots
- 250g small cauliflower florets
- 160g cut green beans,
- 50g finely chopped onion
- 2 tablespoons each: white wine vinegar, brown sugar
- 1–2 tablespoons Curry Seasoning (recipe follows)
- Salt, to taste
- 570g cooked brown rice, warm

INSTRUCTIONS

1. Combine all ingredients, except salt and rice, in a 5 - 6.5 L slow cooker.
2. Cover and cook on low for 6 to 8 hours.
3. Season to taste with salt.
4. Serve with rice.

CURRY SEASONING

MAKES ABOUT 2 TABLESPOONS

INGREDIENTS

- 2 teaspoons ground coriander
- 1 teaspoon ground turmeric, chili powder
- 1/2 teaspoon each: ground cumin, dry mustard, ground ginger, black pepper

INSTRUCTIONS

Combine all ingredients.

EXCLUSIVE BONUS

40 Weight Loss Recipes

&

14 Days Meal Plan

Scan the QR-Code and receive
the FREE download:

PORK

PORK STEW WITH PEPPERS AND ZUCCHINI

TIME: 6-8 HOURS | SERVES 4
NET CARBS: 50G | FAT: 6.1G
PROTEIN: 33G | KCAL: 377

INGREDIENTS

- 500g pork tenderloin or boneless pork loin, cubed
- 1 can (400g) tomato sauce
- 125ml reduced-sodium fat-free chicken broth
- 160g sliced red bell peppers
- 160g sliced green bell peppers
- 1 each: chopped large onion, minced garlic clove
- 3⁄4 teaspoon each: dried basil and thyme leaves
- 1 bay leaf
- 275g thinly sliced zucchini
- 1 tablespoon cornstarch
- 2 tablespoons cold water
- Salt and pepper, to taste
- 200g fusilli, cooked, warm

INSTRUCTIONS

1. Combine all ingredients, except zucchini, cornstarch, water, salt, pepper, and fusilli, in a slow cooker.
2. Cover and cook on high for 3 to 4 hours, adding zucchini during the last 30 minutes.
3. Stir in combined cornstarch and water, stirring, for 2 to 3 minutes.
4. Discard bay leaf.
5. Season to taste with salt and pepper.
6. Serve over fusilli.

BARBECUE PORK STEW

TIME: 6-8 HOURS | SERVES 4
NET CARBS: 82.9G | FAT: 6.4G
PROTEIN: 34G | KCAL: 521

INGREDIENTS

- 500g boneless pork loin, cubed
- 1L cups apple cider or apple juice, divided
- 125ml honey-mustard barbecue sauce
- 360g thinly sliced cabbage
- 1 medium onion, coarsely chopped
- 1 large tart apple, peeled, coarsely chopped
- 1 teaspoon crushed caraway seeds
- 1 tablespoon cornstarch
- 3 tablespoons cold water
- Salt and pepper, to taste
- 200g noodles, cooked, warm

INSTRUCTIONS

1. Combine all ingredients, except cornstarch, water, salt, pepper, and noodles, in a slow cooker.
2. Cover and cook on low for 6 to 8 hours.
3. Turn heat to high and cook for 10 minutes.
4. Stir in combined cornstarch and water, stirring for 2 to 3 minutes.
5. Season to taste with salt and pepper.
6. Serve over noodles.

PORK, POTATO, AND CABBAGE STEW

TIME: 6-8 HOURS | SERVES 4
NET CARBS: 45.4G | FAT: 10G
PROTEIN: 23.4G | KCAL: 328

INGREDIENTS

- 500g boneless lean pork loin
- 1 can (400g) stewed tomatoes
- 60g tomato sauce
- 160g thinly sliced cabbage
- 280g cubed peeled potatoes
- 1 large onion, finely chopped
- 2 cloves garlic, minced
- 1 tablespoon brown sugar
- 2 teaspoons each: balsamic vinegar, dried thyme leaves
- 1 bay leaf
- Salt and pepper, to taste

INSTRUCTIONS

1. Combine all ingredients, except salt and pepper, in a slow cooker.
2. Cover and cook on low for 6 to 8 hours.
3. Discard bay leaf; season to taste with salt and pepper.

SAUSAGE AND BEAN STEW

TIME: 4-5 HOURS | SERVES 8
NET CARBS: 39.4G | FAT: 5.7G
PROTEIN: 19.2G | KCAL: 255

INGREDIENTS

- 500g reduced-fat smoked sausage, sliced
- 2 cans (400g each) light red kidney beans, rinsed, drained
- 1 can (400g) cannellini beans, rinsed, drained
- 2 cans (400g each) diced tomatoes, undrained
- 125ml cup water
- 275g chopped onion
- 50g chopped green bell pepper
- 2 cloves garlic, minced
- 1/2 teaspoon each: dried thyme and savory leaves
- 1 bay leaf
- Salt and pepper, to taste

INSTRUCTIONS

1. Combine all ingredients, except salt and pepper, in a 5 - 6.5 L slow cooker.
2. Cover and cook on high for 4 to 5 hours.
3. Discard bay leaf.
4. Season to taste with salt and pepper.

PULLED PORK SANDWICHES

TIME: 6-8 HOURS | SERVES 12
NET CARBS: 34.9G | FAT: 25.8G
PROTEIN: 20.7G | KCAL: 418

INGREDIENTS

- 1 boneless pork loin roast (about 1kg)
- Brown Sugar Rub (recipe follows)
- 140ml chicken broth
- 12 small buns
- White Barbecue Sauce (recipe follows)

INSTRUCTIONS

1. Rub pork loin with Brown Sugar Rub.
2. Place in a slow cooker with broth.
3. Cover and cook on low for 6 to 8 hours.
4. Remove pork and shred.
5. Reuse cooking liquid for soup or another use.
6. Spoon meat into buns and top with White Barbecue Sauce.

BROWN SUGAR RUB

MAKES ABOUT 50G

INGREDIENTS

- 50g packed light brown sugar
- 1 teaspoon garlic powder
- 1/2 teaspoon each: ground cumin, salt, pepper

INSTRUCTIONS

Mix all ingredients.

WHITE BARBECUE SAUCE

MAKES ABOUT 1200G

INGREDIENTS

- 1200g reduced-fat mayonnaise
- 50ml apple cider vinegar
- 1 tablespoon sugar
- 1 clove garlic, minced
- 2 teaspoons horseradish (optional)
- 1–2 tablespoons lemon juice

INSTRUCTIONS

Mix all ingredients, adding lemon juice to taste.

LAMB

SAVORY LAMB STEW

TIME: 6-8 HOURS | SERVES 6
NET CARBS: 40G | FAT: 10G
PROTEIN: 25G | KCAL: 325

INGREDIENTS

- 450g lamb shanks, fat trimmed
- 1.4 L reduced-sodium fat-free chicken broth
- 1 can (400g) diced tomatoes, undrained
- 100g brown dried lentils
- 70g sliced carrots,
- 70g chopped green bell pepper
- 105g chopped onions
- 2 cloves garlic, minced
- 2 bay leaves
- 2 teaspoons dried thyme leaves
- 1/4 teaspoon each: ground cinnamon and cloves
- Salt and pepper, to taste
- 520g cooked brown rice, warm

INSTRUCTIONS

1. Combine all ingredients, except salt, pepper, and rice, in a 5 - 6.5 L slow cooker.
2. Cover and cook on low for 6 to 8 hours.
3. Discard bay leaves.
4. Remove lamb shanks.
5. Remove lean meat and cut into bite-sized pieces.
6. Return meat to stew.
7. Season to taste with salt and pepper.
8. Serve over rice.

HEARTY ROSEMARY LAMB STEW WITH SWEET POTATOES

TIME: 6-8 HOURS | SERVES 4
NET CARBS: 34.7G | FAT: 9.9G
PROTEIN: 20.6G | KCAL: 285

INGREDIENTS

- 500g boneless lamb shoulder, fat trimmed, cubed
- 750ml cups reduced-sodium fat-free beef broth
- 500g sweet potatoes, peeled, cubed
- 300g cut green beans
- 1 large onion, cut into thin wedges
- 1 teaspoon dried rosemary leaves
- 2 bay leaves
- 1–2 tablespoons cornstarch
- 50ml cold water
- Salt and pepper, to taste

INSTRUCTIONS

1. Combine all ingredients, except cornstarch, water, salt, and pepper, in a slow cooker.
2. Cover and cook on low for 6 to 8 hours.
3. Turn heat to high and cook for 10 minutes.
4. Stir in combined cornstarch and water, stirring for 2 to 3 minutes.
5. Discard bay leaves.
6. Season to taste with salt and pepper.

MOROCCAN LAMB STEW

TIME: 6-8 HOURS | SERVES 8
NET CARBS: 37.4G | FAT: 6.8G
PROTEIN: 23.8G | KCAL: 308

INGREDIENTS

- 500g boneless lean leg of lamb, cubed
- 250ml reduced-sodium fat-free chicken broth
- 275g chopped onions
- 500g chopped tomatoes
- 2 large cloves garlic, minced
- 2 teaspoons minced ginger root
- 1/2 teaspoon ground cinnamon
- 1/4 teaspoon ground turmeric
- 1 bay leaf
- 40g raisins
- Salt and pepper, to taste
- 70g whole almonds, toasted
- 2 hard-cooked eggs, chopped
- Chopped cilantro, as garnish
- 1kg cooked couscous or rice, warm

INSTRUCTIONS

1. Combine all ingredients, except raisins, salt, pepper, almonds, eggs, cilantro, and couscous, in a 5 - 6.5 L slow cooker.
2. Cover and cook on low for 6 to 8 hours, adding raisins during the last 30 minutes.
3. Discard bay leaf, season to taste with salt and pepper.
4. Spoon stew onto a rimmed serving platter.
5. Sprinkle with almonds, hard-cooked eggs, and cilantro.
6. Serve over couscous.

IRISH LAMB STEW

TIME: 6-8 HOURS | SERVES 6
NET CARBS: 38.9G | FAT: 17.2G
PROTEIN: 28G | KCAL: 376

INGREDIENTS

- 2kg lamb cubes for stew
- 500ml reduced-sodium fat-free chicken broth
- 2 medium onions, sliced
- 6 each: quartered medium potatoes, thickly sliced medium carrots
- 1/2 teaspoon dried thyme leaves

- 1 bay leaf
- 160g frozen peas, thawed
- 2 tablespoons cornstarch
- 50ml cold water
- 1–11/2 teaspoons Worcestershire sauce
- Salt and pepper, to taste

INSTRUCTIONS

1. Combine all ingredients, except peas, cornstarch, water, Worcestershire sauce, salt, and pepper, in a slow cooker; cover and cook on low for 6 to 8 hours.
2. Add peas, turn heat to high and cook for 10 minutes.
3. Stir in combined cornstarch and water, stirring for 2 to 3 minutes.
4. Discard bay leaf.
5. Season to taste with Worcestershire sauce, salt, and pepper.

FISH & SEAFOOD

FISH SOUP WITH VEGETABLES

TIME: 6-8 HOURS | SERVES 8
NET CARBS: 25.1G | FAT: 6G
PROTEIN: 20.3G | KCAL: 245

INGREDIENTS

- 2 cans (400g each) crushed tomatoes
- 400ml tomato juice
- 175ml clam juice
- 175ml dry white wine or water
- 50g chopped onion
- 3 medium potatoes, peeled, diced
- 150g chopped celery
- 45g sliced bell pepper,
- 60g sliced carrots
- 60g sliced mushrooms
- 4 cloves garlic, minced
- 1 teaspoon dried oregano leaves
- 200g cubed skinless cod
- 200g cubed skinned sole
- 200g cubed skinned snapper
- Salt and pepper, to taste

INSTRUCTIONS

1. Combine all ingredients, except fish, salt, and pepper, in a 5 - 6.5 L slow cooker.
2. Cover and cook on low for 6 to 8 hours, adding fish during the last 15 to 20 minutes.
3. Season to taste with salt and pepper.

LIGHT SALMON BISQUE WITH DILL

TIME: 6-8 HOURS | SERVES 4
NET CARBS: 22.5G | FAT: 6.9G
PROTEIN: 20.3G | KCAL: 213

INGREDIENTS

- 750 ml Fish Stock or clam juice, divided
- 770g peeled chopped potatoes
- 50g chopped onion
- 25g finely chopped celery
- 55g finely chopped carrot
- 1 tablespoon tomato paste
- 1½ teaspoons dried dill weed
- ¼–½ teaspoon dry mustard
- 200–300g skinless salmon steaks
- 1.3 L whole milk, divided
- 2 tablespoons cornstarch
- 2–3 teaspoons lemon juice
- Salt and white pepper, to taste

INSTRUCTIONS

1. Combine stock, vegetables, tomato paste, dill weed, and dry mustard in a slow cooker.
2. Cover and cook on low for 6 to 8 hours, adding salmon steaks and 500ml milk during the last 15 minutes.
3. Remove the salmon and reserve.
4. Process soup in a food processor or blender until smooth.
5. Return to the slow cooker.
6. Flake reserved salmon into small pieces with a fork.
7. Add to the slow cooker.
8. Cover and cook on high for 10 minutes.
9. Stir in combined remaining milk and cornstarch, stirring for 2 to 3 minutes.
10. Season to taste with lemon juice, salt, and white pepper.

SHRIMP BISQUE

TIME: 4 HOURS | SERVES 4
NET CARBS: 20.8G | FAT: 5G
PROTEIN: 23G | KCAL: 213

INGREDIENTS

- 5.2 L Fish Stock or chicken broth
- 55g tomato paste
- 275g chopped onion
- 3–4 teaspoons curry powder
- 1/2 teaspoon paprika
- 250ml semi-skimmed milk
- 2 tablespoons cornstarch
- 3kg shrimp, peeled, deveined
- 400g cups finely chopped tomatoes
- Salt and cayenne pepper, to taste
- Croutons (optional)

INSTRUCTIONS

1. Combine all ingredients, except shrimp, tomatoes, salt, cayenne pepper, and croutons, in a 5 - 6.5 L slow cooker.
2. Cover and cook on high for 4 hours.
3. Stir in combined milk and cornstarch, stirring for 2 to 3 minutes.
4. Add shrimp and cook for 10 minutes.
5. Process soup in a food processor or blender until smooth.
6. Return to the slow cooker and add tomatoes.
7. Cover and cook on high for 10 minutes.
8. Season to taste with salt and pepper.
9. Sprinkle each bowl of soup with croutons.

SIDES

CHICKEN WINGS

TIME: 3-4 HOURS | SERVES 8
NET CARBS: 4.1G | FAT: 11.8G
PROTEIN: 14G | KCAL: 159

INGREDIENTS

- 4 tablespoons each: margarine or butter, hot pepper sauce
- 1 tablespoon white distilled vinegar

- 3.1 kg (about 16) chicken wings with wing tips removed, halved
- Salt and pepper, to taste
- Blue Cheese Dressing (recipe follows)

INSTRUCTIONS

1. Combine margarine, hot pepper sauce, and vinegar in a slow cooker.
2. Turn heat to high for about 15 minutes and cook until margarine is melted.
3. Sprinkle chicken wings with salt and pepper.
4. Broil 15 cm from heat source until lightly browned, for about 5 minutes on each side.
5. Add to the slow cooker and toss with margarine mixture.
6. Cover and cook on high for 3 to 4 hours.
7. Serve with Blue Cheese Dressing.

BLUE CHEESE DRESSING

MAKES ABOUT 250G

INGREDIENTS

- 170g reduced-fat mayonnaise or salad dressing
- 3 tablespoons crumbled blue cheese
- 11/2 tablespoons red wine vinegar
- 1 teaspoon celery seeds
- 1/2 teaspoon salt
- 1/8 teaspoon each: cayenne and black pepper

INSTRUCTIONS

Mix all ingredients.

ORANGE-GLAZED BABY CARROTS

TIME: 3 HOURS | SERVES 4
NET CARBS: 42.4G | FAT: 3.6G
PROTEIN: 1.8G | KCAL: 191

INGREDIENTS

- 500g baby carrots
- 175ml orange juice
- 1 tablespoon margarine
- 110g packed light brown sugar
- 1/2 teaspoon ground cinnamon
- 1/4 teaspoon ground mace
- 2 tablespoons cornstarch
- 50ml cup water
- Salt and white pepper, to taste

INSTRUCTIONS

1. Combine all ingredients, except cornstarch, water, salt, and white pepper, in a slow cooker.
2. Cover and cook on high until carrots are crisp-tender for about 3 hours.
3. Turn heat to high and cook for 10 minutes.
4. Stir in combined cornstarch and water, stirring for 2 to 3 minutes.
5. Season to taste with salt and pepper.

CAULIFLOWER WITH CREAMY CHEESE SAUCE

TIME: 2 HOURS | SERVES 6
NET CARBS: 11.7G | FAT: 5.1G
PROTEIN: 6.5G | KCAL:102

INGREDIENTS

- 1 medium head cauliflower (500g)
- 1.4 L water
- Creamy Cheese Sauce (recipe follows)
- Paprika, as garnish

INSTRUCTIONS

1. Place cauliflower in a slow cooker and add water.
2. Cover and cook on high for about 2 hours, until cauliflower is tender.
3. Place cauliflower on a serving plate.
4. Spoon Creamy Cheese Sauce over and sprinkle with Paprika.

CREAMY CHEESE SAUCE

MAKES ABOUT 180G

INGREDIENTS

- 2 tablespoons minced onion
- 1 tablespoon margarine or butter
- 2 tablespoons flour
- 250ml semi-skimmed milk
- 115g cubed reduced-fat processed cheese
- 1/4 teaspoon dry mustard
- 2–3 drops red pepper sauce
- Salt and white pepper, to taste

INSTRUCTIONS

1. Sauté onion in margarine in a small saucepan for 2 to 3 minutes.
2. Stir in flour.
3. Cook for 1 minute.
4. Whisk in milk and heat to boiling, stirring until thickened, for about 1 minute.
5. Reduce heat to low.
6. Add cheese, dry mustard, and pepper sauce, whisking until cheese is melted.
7. Season to taste with salt and white pepper.

CREAMY POTATOES AND HAM

TIME: 3-4 HOURS | SERVES 8
NET CARBS: 29G | FAT: 11.9G
PROTEIN: 25.4G | KCAL: 317

INGREDIENTS

- 1 pack (800g) potatoes
- 340g cubed smoked ham
- 1 can (280g) 98% fat-free cream of mushroom soup
- 250ml semi-skimmed milk
- 180g shredded reduced-fat Cheddar cheese
- 1/4 teaspoon pepper

INSTRUCTIONS

1. Combine potatoes and ham in a slow cooker.
2. Mix in the combined remaining ingredients.
3. Cover and cook on high for 3 to 4 hours.

CHEESE FONDUE

TIME: 1- 1 1/2 HOURS | SERVES 12
NET CARBS: 2.8G | FAT: 2.4G
PROTEIN: 7G | KCAL: 83

INGREDIENTS

- 240g shredded reduced-fat Swiss cheese
- 1 tablespoon flour
- 230g reduced-fat cream cheese, room temperature
- 190ml dry white wine or apple juice
- 1 clove garlic, minced
- Cayenne pepper, to taste
- Dippers: cubed French bread, assorted vegetables

INSTRUCTIONS

1. Toss Swiss cheese with flour.
2. Combine cheeses, wine, and garlic in a 1.5 - 3 L slow cooker.
3. Cover and cook for 1 to 1 1/2 hours, until cheeses are melted and fondue is hot.
4. Season to taste with cayenne pepper.
5. Serve with dippers.
6. If fondue becomes too thick, stir in additional wine or milk.

STOCKS & VEGETARIAN SOUPS

CHICKEN STOCK

TIME: 6-8 HOURS | MAKES ABOUT 4L
NET CARBS: 1.3G | FAT: 2G
PROTEIN: 4.9G | KCAL: 83

INGREDIENTS

- 950ml water
- 1.5kg chicken pieces
- 2 ribs celery, thickly sliced
- 3 each: thickly sliced small onions, medium carrots
- 1 small turnip, quartered
- 5 cloves garlic
- 2 bay leaves
- 1/2 teaspoon whole peppercorns
- 1 teaspoon dried sage leaves
- Salt and pepper, to taste

INSTRUCTIONS

1. Combine all ingredients, except salt and pepper, in a slow cooker.
2. Cover and cook on low for 6 to 8 hours.
3. Strain, discarding meat, vegetables, and seasonings.
4. Season to taste with salt and pepper.
5. Refrigerate stock overnight.
6. Skim fat from the surface of the stock.

BEEF STOCK

TIME: 6-8 HOURS | MAKES ABOUT 2L
NET CARBS: 0.9G | FAT: 1.1G
PROTEIN: 2G | KCAL: 29

INGREDIENTS

- 5.5 L water
- 2 ribs from cooked beef rib roast, fat trimmed
- 4 each: thickly sliced large onions, medium carrots, small ribs celery
- 1 parsnip, halved
- 2 bay leaves
- 8 black peppercorns
- 5 sage leaves
- Salt, to taste

INSTRUCTIONS

1. Combine all ingredients, except salt, in a 5 - 6.5 L slow cooker.
2. Cover and cook on low for 6 to 8 hours.
3. Strain stock through a double layer of cheesecloth, discarding solids.
4. Season to taste with salt.
5. Refrigerate until chilled.
6. Remove fat from the surface of the stock.

EASY FISH STOCK

TIME: 4-6 HOURS | MAKES ABOUT 950ML
NET CARBS: 0.2G | FAT: 0G
PROTEIN: 0.7G | KCAL: 10

INGREDIENTS

- 3.8 L water
- 175ml dry white wine or water
- 3kg fresh or frozen fish steaks, cubed
- 1 each: finely chopped medium onion, carrot
- 3 ribs celery with leaves, halved
- 3 sprigs parsley
- 3 slices lemon
- 8 black peppercorns
- Salt, to taste

INSTRUCTIONS

1. Combine all ingredients, except salt, in a slow cooker.
2. Cover and cook on low for 4 to 6 hours.
3. Strain stock through a double layer of cheesecloth, discarding solids.
4. Season to taste with salt.

BASIC VEGETABLE STOCK

TIME: 3-4 HOURS | MAKES ABOUT 2L
NET CARBS: 1G | FAT: 0G
PROTEIN: 0.1G | KCAL: 4

INGREDIENTS

- 2L water
- 250ml dry white wine or water
- 1 each: thickly sliced large onion, leek (white part only), carrot, rib celery
- 400g mixed chopped vegetables (broccoli, green beans, cabbage, potatoes,
- tomatoes, summer or winter squash, bell peppers, mushrooms, etc.)
- 6–8 parsley sprigs
- 1 bay leaf
- 4 whole allspice
- 1 tablespoon black peppercorns
- 2 teaspoons dried bouquet garni
- Salt, to taste

INSTRUCTIONS

1. Combine all ingredients, except salt, in a 5 - 6.5 L slow cooker.
2. Cover and cook on high for 3 to 4 hours or low for 6 to 8 hours.
3. Strain stock, discarding solids.
4. Season to taste with salt.

GARDEN HARVEST SOUP

TIME: 4-6 HOURS | SERVES 6
NET CARBS: 21.3G | FAT: 3.2G
PROTEIN: 8.3G | KCAL: 136

INGREDIENTS

- 2.6 L reduced-sodium fat-free chicken broth
- 150g diced green beans
- 50g diced onion
- 125g diced zucchini
- 140g diced squash
- 70g sliced carrots
- 115g sliced red and yellow bell peppers
- 165g sweetcorn
- 2 cloves garlic, minced
- 1/2 teaspoon each: dried basil and oregano
- 85ml semi-skimmed milk
- Salt and pepper, to taste

INSTRUCTIONS

1. Combine all ingredients, except milk, salt, and pepper, in a 5 - 6.5 L slow cooker.
2. Cover and cook on high for 4 to 6 hours.
3. Add milk during the last 10 minutes.
4. Season to taste with salt and pepper.

TOMATO SOUP WITH PASTA

TIME: 3-4 HOURS | SERVES 6
NET CARBS: 26.3G | FAT: 4.2G
PROTEIN: 7G | KCAL: 164

INGREDIENTS

- 850ml Rich Chicken Stock or chicken broth
- 1.3 kg tomatoes, coarsely chopped
- 25g chopped onions
- 25g chopped carrots
- 125g chopped celery
- 1 clove garlic, minced
- 1 teaspoon each: dried basil and oregano leaves
- 1/2 teaspoon anise seeds, lightly crushed
- 100g small soup pasta (stelline/little stars, orzo, or rings)
- Salt and pepper, to taste
- Shredded Parmesan cheese, as garnish

INSTRUCTIONS

1. Combine all ingredients, except pasta, salt, pepper, and cheese, in a 5 - 6.5 L slow cooker.
2. Cover and cook on high for 3 to 4 hours.
3. Process soup in a food processor or blender until smooth.
4. Return soup to the slow cooker.
5. Cover and cook on high for 10 minutes.
6. Stir in pasta and cook until al dente, for about 20 minutes.
7. Season to taste with salt and pepper.
8. Sprinkle each bowl of soup with Parmesan cheese.

SUMMER SQUASH SOUP

TIME: 4-5 HOURS | SERVES 6
NET CARBS: 20.6G | FAT: 0.9G
PROTEIN: 3.8G | KCAL: 100

INGREDIENTS

- 750ml reduced-sodium fat-free chicken broth
- 4 medium zucchinis, chopped
- 140g peeled cubed potatoes
- 55g chopped shallots
- 15g chopped green onions
- 2 cloves garlic, minced
- 1½ teaspoons dried tarragon leaves
- 230g chopped kale or spinach
- 50–125ml cup semi-skimmed milk
- 1 tablespoon cornstarch
- Salt and white pepper, to taste
- Cayenne pepper, as garnish

INSTRUCTIONS

1. Combine all ingredients, except kale, milk, cornstarch, salt, and white and cayenne pepper, in a slow cooker.
2. Cover and cook on high for 4 to 5 hours, adding kale during the last 15 minutes.
3. Process soup, milk, and cornstarch in a food processor or blender until smooth.
4. Season to taste with salt and white pepper.
5. Serve warm or chilled.
6. Sprinkle each bowl of soup with cayenne pepper.

GINGER PUMPKIN SOUP

TIME: 4-5 HOURS | SERVES 6
NET CARBS: 15.3G | FAT: 0.8G
PROTEIN: 2.8G | KCAL: 83

INGREDIENTS

- 750ml Vegetable Stock
- 1 small pumpkin (about 1kg), peeled, seeded, cubed
- 50g chopped onion
- 1 tablespoon chopped ginger root
- 1 teaspoon minced garlic
- 125ml dry white wine
- 1/2 teaspoon ground cloves
- Salt and pepper, to taste

INSTRUCTIONS

1. Combine all ingredients, except salt and pepper, in a slow cooker.
2. Cover and cook on high for 4 to 5 hours.
3. Process soup in a food processor or blender until smooth.
4. Season to taste with salt and pepper.

GREEN VEGETABLE SOUP

TIME: 4-5 HOURS | SERVES 6
NET CARBS: 26.6G | FAT: 9G
PROTEIN: 6.2G | KCAL: 196

INGREDIENTS

- 950ml vegetable broth
- 70g thinly sliced green cabbage
- 70g chopped celery
- 50g chopped onion
- 50g chopped broccoli florets
- 70g cut green beans,
- 120g cubed zucchini
- 70g potato
- Salt and pepper, to taste
- 60g basil pesto

INSTRUCTIONS

1. Combine all ingredients, except salt, pepper, and pesto, in a slow cooker.
2. Cover and cook on high for 4 to 5 hours.
3. Season to taste with salt and pepper.
4. Stir in basil pesto.

SPICY BARLEY SOUP

TIME: 6-8 HOURS | SERVES 6
NET CARBS: 16.5G | FAT: 3G
PROTEIN: 2.6G | KCAL: 95

INGREDIENTS

- 2L vegetable broth
- 275g chopped onions
- 170g sliced mushrooms
- 60g sliced carrot
- 60g sliced celery
- 70g sliced turnip
- 1 large clove garlic, minced

- 3 tablespoons tomato paste
- 50g pearl barley
- 2 bay leaves
- 1 teaspoon dried marjoram leaves
- 1/2 teaspoon each: dried thyme leaves, celery seeds, dry mustard
- Salt and pepper, to taste

INSTRUCTIONS

1. Combine all ingredients, except salt and pepper, in a 5 - 6.5 L slow cooker.
2. Cover and cook on low for 6 to 8 hours.
3. Discard bay leaves.
4. Season to taste with salt and pepper.

BREADS

BUTTERMILK BREAD

TIME: 2-2 1/2 HOURS | SERVES 8
NET CARBS: 19.5G | FAT: 7.4G
PROTEIN: 1.4G | KCAL: 146

INGREDIENTS

- 690g all-purpose flour
- 2 teaspoons baking powder
- 1/8 teaspoon baking soda
- 1/2 teaspoon salt
- 4 tablespoons cold margarine or butter, cut into pieces
- 180ml low-fat buttermilk
- 1 tablespoon dried parsley

INSTRUCTIONS

1. Combine flour, baking powder, baking soda, and salt in a bowl.
2. Cut in margarine until the mixture resembles small crumbs.
3. Stir in buttermilk and parsley.
4. Knead dough on a floured surface for 1 to 2 minutes.
5. Pat dough into a greased 7-inch (18cm) springform pan and place on a rack in a 5 - 6.5 L slow cooker.
6. Cover and cook on high for 2 to 2 1/2 hours, until a toothpick inserted in the centre comes out clean.
7. Cool in the pan on a wire rack for 10 minutes.
8. Remove the side of the pan.
9. Break off pieces to serve.

BROWN SUGAR BANANA BREAD

TIME: 2-3 HOURS | SERVES 16
NET CARBS: 23.7G | FAT: 4.9G
PROTEIN: 1.6G | KCAL: 146

INGREDIENTS

- 4 tablespoons margarine or butter, room temperature
- 60g applesauce
- 2 eggs
- 2 tablespoons semi-skimmed milk or water
- 150g packed light brown sugar
- 2–3 medium mashed ripe bananas
- 450g all-purpose flour
- 2 teaspoons baking powder
- 1/2 teaspoon baking soda
- 1/4 teaspoon salt
- 25g coarsely chopped walnuts or pecans

INSTRUCTIONS

1. Beat margarine, applesauce, eggs, milk, and brown sugar in a large bowl until smooth.
2. Add bananas and mix at low speed.
3. Beat at high speed for 1 to 2 minutes.
4. Mix in combined flour, baking powder, baking soda, and salt.
5. Mix in walnuts.
6. Pour batter into a greased 9 x 5-inch (23 x 13 cm) loaf pan.
7. Place the pan on a rack in a 5 - 6.5 L slow cooker.
8. Cover and cook on high for 2 to hours, until a toothpick inserted in the centre of the bread comes out clean.
9. Cool in a pan on a wire rack for 5 minutes.
10. Remove bread from the pan and cool on a wire rack.

FRUIT AND NUT BANANA BREAD

TIME: 3 1/2 HOURS | SERVES 12
NET CARBS: 27.9G | FAT: 11.7G
PROTEIN: 3.5G | KCAL: 211

INGREDIENTS

- 6 tablespoons margarine or butter, room temperature
- 100g sugar
- 2 eggs
- 450g mashed ripe bananas
- 400g self-rising flour
- 1/2 teaspoon salt
- 60g chopped dried apples
- 65g chopped pecans

INSTRUCTIONS

1. Beat margarine and sugar in a large bowl until fluffy.
2. Beat in eggs and bananas.
3. Mix in flour and salt.
4. Mix in dried apples and pecans.
5. Pour batter into a greased 9 x 5-inch (23 x 13 cm) loaf pan.
6. Place on a rack in a 5 - 6.5 L slow cooker.
7. Cover and cook on high for about 3 1/2 hours, until a wooden skewer inserted in the centre of bread comes out clean.
8. Cool on a wire rack for 5 minutes.
9. Remove from the pan and cool.

PARMESAN BREAD

TIME: 2 HOURS | SERVES 6-8
NET CARBS: 23.9G | FAT: 17.7G
PROTEIN: 6G | KCAL: 249

INGREDIENTS

- 1 small loaf of Italian bread (about 300g)
- 6 tablespoons margarine or butter, room temperature
- 30g grated Parmesan cheese

INSTRUCTIONS

1. Cut bread into 6 to 8 slices, cutting to but not through the bottom of the loaf.
2. Spread both sides of bread slices with combined margarine and Parmesan cheese.
3. Wrap loaf securely in aluminum foil.
4. Place in a 5 - 6.5 L slow cooker and cook on low for 2 hours.

DRINKS

HOT CHOCOLATE

TIME: 2 HOURS | SERVES 12
NET CARBS: 17.9G | FAT: 5.6G
PROTEIN: 6G | KCAL: 144

INGREDIENTS

- 60g dark cocoa powder
- 100g sugar
- 1/2 teaspoon ground cinnamon
- Pinch salt
- 2.9 L whole milk
- 1/2 teaspoon vanilla

INSTRUCTIONS

1. Combine cocoa, sugar, cinnamon, and salt in a slow cooker.
2. Whisk in enough milk to make a smooth paste.
3. Whisk in remaining milk and vanilla.
4. Cover and cook on high until hot and steaming (do not boil) for about 2 hours.
5. Turn heat to low to keep warm for serving.
6. Add marshmallows or dollops of marshmallow crème to each cup of Hot Chocolate.

SPICED WHITE CHOCOLATE

TIME: 2 HOURS | SERVES 12
NET CARBS: 19.6G | FAT: 19.7G
PROTEIN: 7G | KCAL: 219

INGREDIENTS

- 880g white chocolate chips
- 2L whole milk
- 1/4 teaspoon each: ground cinnamon and nutmeg

INSTRUCTIONS

1. Place chocolate chips in a slow cooker.
2. Cover and cook on low for about 30 minutes, until chocolate is melted.
3. Gradually whisk in milk and spices.
4. Cover and cook on high for about 2 hours, until hot and steaming (do not boil).
5. Turn heat to low to keep warm for serving.

HOT GINGER LEMONADE

TIME: 2-3 HOURS | SERVES 12
NET CARBS: 13.9G | FAT: 0G
PROTEIN: 0G | KCAL: 53

INGREDIENTS

- 1.2 L water
- 175ml lemon juice
- 150g sugar
- 2-inch piece ginger root, sliced

INSTRUCTIONS

1. Combine all ingredients in a slow cooker.
2. Cover and cook on high for 2 to 3 hours (if mixture begins to boil, turn heat to low).
3. Turn to low to keep warm for serving.

HONEY CHAI

TIME: 2 HOURS | SERVES 12
NET CARBS: 13.9G | FAT: 3.1G
PROTEIN: 1G | KCAL: 69

INGREDIENTS

- 5 L quarts water
- 500ml whole milk
- 2 cinnamon sticks
- 1 teaspoon ground cardamom
- 1-inch piece ginger root, sliced
- 120g honey
- 12 black tea bags or 50ml loose black tea

INSTRUCTIONS

1. Combine all ingredients in a slow cooker.
2. Cover and cook on high for about 2 hours, until hot and steaming (do not boil).
3. Remove tea bags and ginger root with a slotted spoon.
4. Turn heat to low to keep warm for serving.

DESSERTS

CHOCOLATE-COFFEE CAKE

TIME: 2 1/2 HOURS | SERVES 12
NET CARBS: 34.4G | FAT: 8.1G
PROTEIN: 2.8G | KCAL: 208

INGREDIENTS

- 6 tablespoons margarine or butter, room temperature
- 750g sugar
- 2 eggs
- 125g all-purpose flour
- 40g dark cocoa powder
- 1/2 teaspoon baking soda
- 1/4 teaspoon each: baking powder, salt
- 1–2 tablespoons each: instant espresso or coffee, boiling water
- 80g reduced-fat sour cream
- Coffee Glaze (recipe follows)

INSTRUCTIONS

1. Beat margarine and sugar in a bowl until fluffy.
2. Beat in eggs one at a time, beating well after each addition.
3. Mix in combined dry ingredients alternately with combined espresso, boiling water, and sour cream, beginning and ending with dry ingredients.
4. Pour batter into a greased and floured 6-cup fluted cake pan.
5. Place the pan on a rack in a 5 - 6.5 L slow cooker.
6. Cover and cook on high for 4 to 4 1/2 hours, until a toothpick inserted in the centre of the cake comes out clean.
7. Cool cake on a wire rack for 10 minutes.
8. Drizzle cake with Coffee Glaze.

COFFEE GLAZE

MAKES ABOUT 100G

INGREDIENTS

- 85g powdered sugar
- 1 tablespoon margarine or butter, melted
- 2-3 tablespoons strong brewed coffee

INSTRUCTIONS

Mix powdered sugar, margarine, and enough coffee to make glaze consistency.

SWEET POTATO PUDDING

TIME: 3 HOURS | SERVES 6
NET CARBS: 27.7G | FAT: 3.8G
PROTEIN: 5.5G | KCAL: 179

INGREDIENTS

- Vegetable cooking spray
- 4 medium sweet potatoes, peeled, cubed
- 50ml orange juice
- 1–2 tablespoons margarine or butter
- 55g packed light brown sugar
- 1 tablespoon grated orange zest
- 1/4 teaspoon each: ground cinnamon, cloves, salt
- 3 eggs, lightly beaten
- 50g miniature marshmallows

INSTRUCTIONS

1. Spray the bottom and side of a slow cooker with cooking spray and add sweet potatoes.
2. Cover and cook on high for about 3 hours, until potatoes are tender.
3. Remove the potatoes and mash with remaining ingredients, except eggs and marshmallows.
4. Mix in eggs.
5. Return potatoes to slow cooker.
6. Cover and cook on high for 30 minutes, sprinkling with marshmallows during the last 5 minutes.

LEMONY CARROT CAKE WITH CREAM CHEESE GLAZE

TIME: 3 1/2 HOURS | SERVES 12
NET CARBS: 44.3G | FAT: 16.6G
PROTEIN: 4.5G | KCAL: 337

INGREDIENTS

- 12 tablespoons margarine or butter, at room temperature
- 165g packed light brown sugar
- 3 eggs
- 180g shredded carrots
- 50g raisins
- 50g coarsely chopped walnuts
- Grated zest of 1 lemon
- 690g self-rising flour
- 1 teaspoon baking powder
- 1/4 teaspoon salt
- Cream Cheese Glaze (recipe follows)

INSTRUCTIONS

1. Beat margarine and brown sugar in a large bowl until fluffy; beat in eggs one at a time.
2. Mix in carrots, raisins, walnuts, and lemon zest.
3. Fold in combined flour, baking powder and salt.
4. Pour batter into greased and floured 7-cup springform pan.
5. Place on a rack in a slow cooker.
6. Cover and cook on high for about 3 1/2 hours, until a toothpick inserted in the centre of the cake comes out clean.
7. Cool pan on a wire rack for 10 minutes.
8. Remove the side of the pan and cool.
9. Drizzle cake with Cream Cheese Glaze.

CREAM CHEESE GLAZE

MAKES ABOUT 225G

INGREDIENTS

- 50g reduced-fat cream cheese, room temperature
- 1 tablespoon margarine or butter, room temperature
- 1/2 teaspoon vanilla
- 620g cups powdered sugar
- Milk

INSTRUCTIONS

1. Beat cream cheese, margarine, and vanilla in a medium bowl until smooth.
2. Beat in powdered sugar and enough milk to make thick glaze consistency.

GINGERBREAD CAKE

TIME: 5 HOURS | SERVES 12
NET CARBS: 53.4G | FAT: 12.4G
PROTEIN: 2.8G | KCAL: 315

INGREDIENTS

- 690g self-rising flour
- 60g all-purpose flour
- 1 teaspoon ground cinnamon
- 1/2 teaspoon ground ginger
- 1/4 teaspoon each: ground allspice, salt
- 8 tablespoons margarine or butter, room temperature
- 190g light molasses
- 165g cup packed light brown sugar
- 1 egg, lightly beaten
- 125ml semi-skimmed milk
- 1/2 teaspoon baking soda
- Cream Cheese Glaze (recipe follows)

INSTRUCTIONS

1. Combine flours, spices, and salt in a large bowl.
2. Combine margarine, molasses, and brown sugar in a 1L glass measuring cup.
3. Microwave on high until margarine is melted, about 2 minutes, stirring to blend.
4. Whisk margarine mixture into the flour mixture, blending well.
5. Whisk in egg.
6. Whisk in combined milk and baking soda until blended.
7. Pour batter into a greased and floured 7-inch (18cm) springform pan.
8. Place on rack in a slow cooker.
9. Cover and cook on high for about 5 hours, until a toothpick inserted in the centre of the cake comes out clean.
10. Cool in the pan on a wire rack for 10 minutes.
11. Remove the side of the pan and cool.
12. Drizzle with Cream Cheese Glaze.

CREAM CHEESE GLAZE

MAKES ABOUT 225G

INGREDIENTS

- 50g reduced-fat cream cheese, room temperature
- 1 tablespoon margarine or butter, room temperature
- 1/2 teaspoon vanilla
- 620g cups powdered sugar
- Milk

INSTRUCTIONS

1. Beat cream cheese, margarine, and vanilla in a medium bowl until smooth.
2. Beat in powdered sugar and enough milk to make thick glaze consistency.

RED VELVET CAKE

TIME: 2-2 3/4 HOURS | SERVES 8
NET CARBS: 48.8G | FAT: 7.9G
PROTEIN: 3.4G | KCAL: 265

INGREDIENTS

- 150g sugar
- 3 tablespoons vegetable shortening
- 1 egg
- 1 teaspoon vanilla
- 1 bottle (28g) red food colouring
- 30g unsweetened cocoa
- 140g all-purpose flour
- 1 teaspoon baking soda
- 1/2 teaspoon salt
- 125ml low-fat buttermilk
- 30ml white distilled vinegar
- Buttercream Frosting (recipe follows)

INSTRUCTIONS

1. Beat sugar and shortening until well blended in a large bowl.
2. Add the egg and vanilla, blending well.
3. Beat in food colouring and cocoa until well blended.
4. Mix in combined flour, baking soda, and salt alternately with combined buttermilk and vinegar, beginning and ending with dry ingredients.
5. Pour batter into greased and floured 1 L soufflé dish.
6. Place on a rack in a 5 - 6.5 L slow cooker.
7. Cover and cook on high for 2 to 2 3/4 hours, until a toothpick inserted in the centre of the cake comes out clean.
8. Remove the wire rack and cool for 10 minutes.
9. Invert onto a rack and cool.
10. Frost with Buttercream Frosting.

BUTTERCREAM FROSTING

MAKES ABOUT 500G

INGREDIENTS

- 500g powdered sugar
- 1 tablespoon margarine or butter, room temperature
- 1/2 teaspoon vanilla
- 1–2 tablespoons milk

INSTRUCTIONS

1. Mix powdered sugar, margarine, vanilla, and enough milk to make spreading consistency.

CHOCOLATE CHIP PEANUT BUTTER CAKE

TIME: 2-2 3/4 HOURS | SERVES 8
NET CARBS: 36.4G | FAT: 27.3G
PROTEIN: 7.4G | KCAL: 352

INGREDIENTS

- 230g room temperature margarine or butter
- 70g granulated and packed light brown sugar
- 2 eggs
- 120g chunky peanut butter,
- 120g reduced-fat sour cream
- 500g cups self-rising flour
- 1/4 teaspoon salt
- 80g semi-sweet chocolate chip
- Hot fudge or chocolate sauce (optional)

INSTRUCTIONS

1. Beat margarine and sugars in the bowl until fluffy.
2. Beat in eggs, blending well.
3. Mix in peanut butter and sour cream.
4. Mix in flour, salt, and chocolate chips.
5. Pour batter into greased and floured 1.5 L fluted cake pan.
6. Place on a rack in a 5 - 6.5 L slow cooker. Cover and cook on high for 2 to 2 1/2 hours, until a toothpick inserted in the centre of the cake comes out clean.
7. Cool cake on a wire rack for 10 minutes.
8. Invert onto rack and cool.
9. Serve with hot fudge sauce.

HOT FUDGE PUDDING CAKE

TIME: 2 HOURS | SERVES 6
NET CARBS: 36.6G | FAT: 40.6G
PROTEIN: 2.9G | KCAL: 192

INGREDIENTS

- 125g all-purpose flour
- 100g packed light brown sugar
- 6 tablespoons dark cocoa powder, divided
- 5 1/2 teaspoons baking powder
- 1/4 teaspoon salt

- 125ml semi-skimmed milk
- 2 tablespoons vegetable oil
- 1 teaspoon vanilla
- 70g granulated sugar
- 1.4 L boiling water

INSTRUCTIONS

1. Wrap the bottom of a springform pan in aluminum foil.
2. Combine flour, brown sugar, 3 tablespoons cocoa, baking powder, and salt in a medium bowl.
3. Whisk combined milk, oil, and vanilla into the flour mixture, mixing well.
4. Spoon batter into greased 7-inch (18cm) springform pan.
5. Mix remaining 3 tablespoons cocoa and granulated sugar.
6. Sprinkle over cake batter.
7. Slowly pour boiling water over the back of a large spoon or spatula over the batter. Do not stir.
8. Place the pan on a rack in a 1.5 - 3 L slow cooker.
9. Cover and cook on high for about 2 hours, until the cake springs back when touched.
10. Cool pan on a wire rack for 10 minutes.
11. Remove the side of the pan and serve warm.

NEW YORK-STYLE CHEESECAKE

TIME: 12 HOURS | SERVES 8
NET CARBS: 35.4G | FAT: 52.4G
PROTEIN: 10.1G | KCAL: 335

INGREDIENTS

- 500g reduced-fat cream cheese, room temperature
- 100g cup sugar
- 2 eggs
- 5 1/2 tablespoons cornstarch
- 1/4 teaspoon salt
- 185g reduced-fat sour cream
- 1 teaspoon vanilla
- Graham Cracker Crumb Crust (recipe follows)

INSTRUCTIONS

1. Beat cream cheese and sugar in a large bowl until light and fluffy.
2. Beat in eggs, cornstarch, and salt, blending well.
3. Mix in sour cream and vanilla.
4. Pour into the crust in a springform pan.
5. Place the pan on a rack in a 5 - 6.5 L slow cooker.
6. Cover, placing 3 layers of paper towels under the lid, and cook on high for 2 to 3 hours, until the cheesecake is set, but still slightly soft in the centre.
7. Turn off heat and let stand, covered, in the slow cooker for 1 hour. Remove from the slow cooker and cool on the wire rack.
8. Refrigerate, covered, for 8 hours or overnight.

GRAHAM CRACKER CRUMB CRUST

MAKES ONE 18CM CRUST

INGREDIENTS

- 275g cups graham cracker crumbs
- 2 tablespoons sugar
- 3 tablespoons margarine or butter, melted
- 1–2 tablespoons honey

INSTRUCTIONS

1. Combine graham crumbs, sugar, and margarine in a 7-inch (18cm) springform pan.
2. Add enough honey for mixture to stick together.
3. Pat mixture evenly on the bottom and 3cm up the side of the pan.

CHOCOLATE CHIP BAR COOKIES

TIME: 3-3 1/2 HOURS | SERVES 16
NET CARBS: 17.6G | FAT: 13.2G
PROTEIN: 1.4G | KCAL: 169

INGREDIENTS

- 8 tablespoons margarine or butter, room temperature
- 1 egg
- 1 teaspoon vanilla
- 50g granulated sugar
- 50g packed light brown sugar
- 125g all-purpose flour
- 1/2 teaspoon baking soda
- 1/4 teaspoon salt
- 80g semi-sweet chocolate chips
- 80g coarsely chopped walnuts
- Vegetable cooking spray

INSTRUCTIONS

1. Beat margarine, egg, and vanilla in a bowl until fluffy.
2. Mix in combined sugars.
3. Mix in combined flour, baking soda, and salt.
4. Mix in chocolate chips and walnuts.
5. Spread dough evenly on the bottom of a greased 7-inch (18cm) springform pan.
6. Cover and cook on high in a slow cooker for 3 to 3 1/2 hours, until a toothpick inserted in the centre comes out clean.
7. Turn lid askew and cook for 20 minutes longer.
8. Cool in a pan on a wire rack for 5 minutes.
9. Remove the side of the pan.
10. Cut into bars while warm.

EASY BROWNIES

TIME: 6 HOURS | SERVES 16
NET CARBS: 34.4G | FAT: 14.7G
PROTEIN: 3.1G | KCAL: 249

INGREDIENTS

- 1 pack (500g) brownie mix
- 4 tablespoons margarine or butter, melted
- 80–160g chopped walnuts

INSTRUCTIONS

1. Make brownie mix according to pack directions, adding margarine and walnuts.
2. Pour batter in a greased 7-inch (18cm) springform pan and place on rack in a 5 - 6.5 L slow cooker.
3. Cover and cook on high for about 6 hours, until a toothpick inserted in centre comes out
4. almost clean.
5. Cool on a wire rack.
6. Remove the side of the pan and cut into squares or wedges.

CARAMEL FLAN

TIME: 9 ½- 10 HOURS | SERVES 4-6
NET CARBS: 22.7G | FAT: 10.3G
PROTEIN: 7.9G | KCAL: 186

INGREDIENTS

- 200g sugar, divided
- 625ml whole milk
- 3 eggs, lightly beaten
- 2 teaspoons vanilla

INSTRUCTIONS

1. Heat 100g sugar in a small skillet over medium-high heat until the sugar melts and turns golden, stirring occasionally.
2. Quickly pour the syrup into the bottom of 1L soufflé dish or casserole and tilt the bottom to spread the caramel.
3. Set aside to cool.
4. Heat milk and remaining 100g sugar until steaming and just beginning to bubble at the edges.
5. Whisk mixture into eggs.
6. Add vanilla.
7. Strain into soufflé dish over caramel.
8. Place soufflé dish on rack in a 5 - 6.5 L slow cooker.
9. Add 2.5cm hot water to the slow cooker and cover the dish with a plate, lid, or aluminum foil.
10. Cover and cook on low for 1 1/2 to 2 hours, until custard is set and a sharp knife inserted halfway between centre and edge comes out clean.
11. Remove soufflé dish to wire rack, uncover, and cool.
12. Refrigerate for 8 hours or overnight.
13. To unmold, loosen the edge of custard with a sharp knife.
14. Place rimmed serving dish over soufflé dish and invert.

CREAMY RICE PUDDING

TIME: 2 HOURS | SERVES 6
NET CARBS: 44.5G | FAT: 8.5G
PROTEIN: 6.8G | KCAL: 255

INGREDIENTS

- 950ml whole milk, divided
- 70g sugar
- 1/2 teaspoon salt
- 150g converted long-grain rice, cooked
- 5 1/2 tablespoons cornstarch
- Ground cinnamon, as garnish

INSTRUCTIONS

1. Heat 750ml milk, sugar, and salt to boiling in a medium saucepan.
2. Combine with rice in a slow cooker.
3. Stir in combined remaining 250ml milk and cornstarch.
4. Cover and cook on high for 2 hours, until pudding is thick and creamy.
5. Serve warm or refrigerate and serve cold.
6. Sprinkle with cinnamon.

CRANBERRY-APPLE TART

TIME: 3 HOURS | SERVES 8
NET CARBS: 35.3G | FAT: 7.7G
PROTEIN: 5.2G | KCAL: 216

INGREDIENTS

- Frozen pastry for 22.5cm pie crust, thawed
- 150g sugar
- 2 tablespoons flour
- 75ml water
- 2 teaspoons grated orange zest
- 1/8 teaspoon ground nutmeg
- 525g peeled sliced apples
- 130g fresh or frozen cranberries
- Powdered sugar, as garnish

INSTRUCTIONS

1. Roll pastry on a floured surface into a 10-inch (25cm) round.
2. Fit into the bottom and 14cm up the side of a 7-inch (18cm) springform pan.
3. Bake for about 15 minutes at 190 degrees until lightly browned.
4. Mix sugar and flour in a large saucepan.
5. Add water, orange zest, and nutmeg.
6. Heat to boiling, stirring to dissolve the sugar.
7. Add apples and cranberries.
8. Simmer for 10 minutes or until cranberries pop, stirring occasionally.
9. Spoon fruit mixture into the crust, spreading evenly.
10. Place the pan on the rack in a 5 - 6.5 L slow cooker.
11. Cover and cook on high for 2 1/2 hours.
12. Cool on a wire rack.
13. Sprinkle it with powdered sugar before serving.

BAKED STUFFED APPLES

TIME: 1 ½-2 HOURS | SERVES 4
NET CARBS: 44G | FAT: 10.1G
PROTEIN: 1.2G | KCAL: 241

INGREDIENTS

- 4 medium baking apples
- 150g chopped mixed dried fruit
- 2–4 tablespoons chopped toasted pecans
- 3 tablespoons sugar
- 1/2 teaspoon ground cinnamon
- 1/8 teaspoon ground nutmeg
- 2–3 tablespoons cold margarine, cut into pieces

INSTRUCTIONS

1. Core apples, cutting to, but not through, the bottoms.
2. Peel 2.5cm of the skin from the tops.
3. Fill apples with the combined remaining ingredients and place in a slow cooker.
4. Cover and cook on high for 1 1/2 - 2 hours until tender.

CHOCOLATE FONDUE

TIME: ½ - ¾ HOURS | SERVES 16
NET CARBS: 34,1G | FAT: 20.2G
PROTEIN: 3.4G | KCAL: 314

INGREDIENTS

- 960g dark chocolate, coarsely chopped
- 180–240g half-and-half or light cream
- 3–4 tablespoons rum or brandy (optional)
- Dippers: whole strawberries, fruit pieces, angel food cake

INSTRUCTIONS

1. Combine chocolate and half-and-half in a 1.5 - 3 L slow cooker.
2. Cover and cook for 30 to 45 minutes, until the chocolate is melted.
3. Whisk in rum.
4. Serve with dippers.

BONUS: 30-Day Slow Cooker Dinner Meal Plan

Days 1 - 7

Menu

Family Beef Stew
Honey-Mustard Chicken Stew
Irish Lamb Stew
Fish Soup with Vegetables
Indian Curry Chicken and Vegetable Stew
Moroccan Lamb Stew
Green Vegetable Soup

Shopping List

- 500g beef round steak
- 450g boneless, skinless chicken breast
- 2kg lamb cubes
- 500g boneless lean leg of lamb, cubed
- 500g chicken breasts
- 200g cubed skinless cod
- 200g cubed skinned sole
- 200g cubed skinned snapper

- Reduced-sodium fat-free chicken broth
- Reduced-sodium fat-free beef broth
- Green beans
- Medium potatoes
- Onions
- Carrots
- Celery
- Mushrooms
- Garlic
- Ginger root

- Small cauliflower florets
- Frozen peas
- Cabbage
- Celery
- Zucchini
- Raisins
- Whole almonds
- Eggs
- Cilantro
- Canned tomatoes
- Tomato juice
- Tomato paste

- Clam juice
- Basil pesto

Already have?
- Dried thyme leaves
- Bay leaf
- Oregano leaves
- Ground cinnamon
- Ground turmeric

- Reduced-fat or regular coconut milk

- Honey
- Dijon mustard
- Worcestershire sauce
- White wine vinegar
- Brown sugar

- White rice
- Couscous

- Curry Powder
- Cornstarch
- Salt
- Pepper

Days 8 - 14

Menu
Greek Beef and Lentil Stew
Chicken and Mushroom Stew
Sausage and Bean Stew
Savory Lamb Stew
Light Salmon Bisque with Dill
Lemon Chicken Stew
Garden Harvest Soup

Shopping List
- 500g cubed boneless beef
- 500g boneless, skinless chicken breast
- 500g reduced-fat smoked sausage
- 200-300g skinless salmon steaks

- 500g boneless, skinless chicken breast
- Reduced-sodium fat-free chicken broth
- Reduced-sodium fat-free beef broth
- Potatoes
- Green beans

- Onions
- Zucchini
- Green bell pepper
- Garlic
- Dried lentils
- Mint leaves
- Tomato paste
- Mushrooms

- Celery
- Onions
- Garlic
- Broccoli florets
- Carrots
- Green beans
- Zucchini
- Squash

- Red and yellow bell peppers
- Sweetcorn
- Canned tomatoes
- Tomato paste
- Spaghetti
- Canned kidney beans
- Canned cannellini beans
- Dried dill weed

- Whole milk
- Lemon juice
- Jalapeño chili
- Instant chicken bouillon crystals
- Angel hair pasta
- Parmesan cheese
- Semi-skimmed milk

Already have?
- Bay leaf
- Dried oregano
- Dried basil leaves
- Ground turmeric
- Dried thyme

- Ground coriander
- Worcestershire sauce
- Mustard
- Italian seasoning
- Mustard

- Cornstarch
- Salt
- Pepper

Days 15 - 21

Menu
Chili con Carne
Chicken and Mashed Potato Stew
Tomato-Chicken Stew
Pork Stew with Peppers and Zucchini
Shrimp Bisque
Taco Chili
Summer Squash Soup

Shopping List
- 450g lean minced beef

- 250 - 500g lean minced beef
- 500g boneless, skinless chicken breast
- 500g pork tenderloin or boneless pork loin
- 3kg boneless, skinless chicken breast
- 3kg shrimp
- Reduced-sodium fat-free chicken broth
- Reduced-sodium fat-free beef broth
- Onions
- Potatoes
- Green bell pepper
- Garlic
- Green onions
- Red and green bell peppers
- Carrots
- Zucchini

- Celery
- Shallots
- Green onions
- Mushrooms
- Sweetcorn
- Kale/Spinach
- Canned tomatoes
- Canned cannellini beans
- Canned red kidney beans
- Frozen peas
- Egg
- Margarine/Butter
- Tomato paste
- Unsweetened cocoa
- Cheddar cheese
- Reduced-fat sour cream
- Lemon Juice
- Fusilli pasta
- Semi-skimmed milk
- Croutons
- Taco seasoning mix
- Ranch seasoning mix

- Sour cream
- Cheddar cheese
- Taco chips
- *Already have?*
- Chili powder
- Ground cumin
- Dried oregano leaves
- Dried tarragon leaves
- Bay leaf
- Dried rosemary
- Dried thyme leaves
- Curry powder
- Paprika
- Light brown sugar
- Cornstarch
- Cayenne pepper
- Cornstarch
- White pepper
- Salt
- Pepper

Days 22 - 30

Menu
Beef and Vegetable Stew
Classic Chicken Noodle Soup
Beef Stroganoff
Pork, Potato, and Cabbage Stew

Easy Chicken Stew
Hearty Meatball & Veggie Stew
Tomato Soup with Pasta
Sloppy Joes
Pulled Pork Sandwiches

Shopping List

- 3kg lean beef round steak
- 500g lean beef eye of round or sirloin steak
- 500g minced beef
- 600g boneless, skinless chicken breast
- 100g skinless chicken thighs
- 1.5kg boneless lean pork loin
- Reduced-sodium fat-free chicken broth
- Reduced-sodium fat-free beef broth
- Reduced-sodium 98% fat-free condensed cream of chicken soup
- Carrots
- Onions
- Potatoes
- Onions
- Celery
- Zucchini
- Mushrooms
- Green bell pepper

- Cabbage
- Tomatoes
- Garlic
- Frozen mixed vegetables
- Frozen peas
- Canned tomatoes
- Wide noodles
- Reduced-fat sour cream
- Noodles
- Semi-skimmed milk
- Small soup pasta (stelline/little stars, orzo, or rings)
- Parmesan cheese
- Whole-wheat hamburger buns
- Small buns
- Sweet or dill pickles
- Lemon juice
- *Already have?*
- Ketchup
- Mayonnaise
- Apple cider vinegar
- Light brown sugar
- Ground cumin

- Mustard
- Chili powder
- Celery seeds
- Bay leaves
- Anise seeds
- Dried marjoram leaves
- Dried thyme leaves
- Dried basil leaves
- Brown sugar
- Balsamic vinegar
- Worcestershire sauce
- Dijon mustard
- Cornstarch
- Salt
- Pepper

EXCLUSIVE BONUS

40 Weight Loss Recipes

&

14 Days Meal Plan

Scan the QR-Code and receive
the FREE download:

Disclaimer

This book contains opinions and ideas of the author and is meant to teach the reader informative and helpful knowledge while due care should be taken by the user in the application of the information provided. The instructions and strategies are possibly not right for every reader and there is no guarantee that they work for everyone. Using this book and implementing the information/recipes therein contained is explicitly your own responsibility and risk. This work with all its contents, does not guarantee correctness, completion, quality or correctness of the provided information. Misinformation or misprints cannot be completely eliminated.

Printed in Great Britain
by Amazon

11415786R00064